Information Systems Engineering Library

Quality Management for PRINCE and SSADM Projects

Ian Drummond

CCTA
February 1993
LONDON: HMSO

© Crown Copyright 1993

Applications for reproduction should be made to HMSO

First published 1993

ISBN 0 11 330580 X
ISSN 0967-9561

For further information regarding this publication and other CCTA products please contact:

CCTA Library
Riverwalk House
157-161 Millbank
London SW1P 4RT

071-217-3331

Contents

Foreword

1	**Introduction**		1
	1.1	Purpose	
	1.2	Who should read this volume	
	1.3	Structure of this volume	
	1.4	How to use this volume	
2	**Quality Management for IS Development Projects**		5
	2.1	The importance of quality in IS development	
	2.2	Quality system framework	
	2.3	Quality standards	
	2.4	Certification	
	2.5	TickIT accreditation	
	2.6	Definitions and terminology	
3	**PRINCE and SSADM within a Quality System**		13
	3.1	Introduction	
	3.2	PRINCE	
	3.3	SSADM	
	3.4	Summary	
4	**The Requirements of ISO 9001**		19

Annex	The Relationship of PRINCE and SSADM to ISO 9001	61
Bibliography		67
Glossary		69

Foreword

The **Information Systems Engineering Library** provides guidance on carrying out Information Systems Engineering activities. In the IS life cycle, Information Systems Engineering takes place once the IS strategy has been defined. It is concerned with the development of information systems up to the operational stage, when an information system becomes the responsibility of infrastructure management.

The Information Systems Engineering Library builds on the guidance in the CCTA IS Guides B set: *Systems Development Set* and complements other CCTA products, in particular the IS project management method, PRINCE, and the systems analysis and design method, SSADM.

The Information Systems Engineering Library is of interest to IS providers, helping them to improve the quality and productivity of their IS development work. It is also of interest to business managers, whose business operations depend on having effective IS support by means of Information Systems Engineering activities.

CCTA welcomes customer views on Information Systems Engineering Library publications. Please send your comments to:

> Customer Services
> Information Systems Engineering Group
> CCTA
> Gildengate House
> Upper Green Lane
> Norwich NR3 1DW

Acknowledgements

This volume is based on a document produced for CCTA by David Hawkins, quality manager for Pacific Associates Ltd. Further information on SSADM was contributed by Admiral Management Services Ltd.

In preparation of this volume, reference has been made to the Guide to Software Quality Management System Construction and Certification using EN 29001 (TickIT manual).

Extracts from ISO 9001 and BS 7000 are reproduced with permission from the British Standards Institute.

1 Introduction

1.1 Purpose

The purpose of this volume is:

- to explain to providers of information systems (IS) how they can conform to the requirements of the international quality standard ISO 9001 on projects that use PRINCE and SSADM, thereby improving their own quality management

- to help customers in the appraisal of their IS suppliers' quality systems.

The volume describes which requirements of ISO 9001 are met by the use of PRINCE and SSADM and the additional measures required to satisfy those requirements in projects which use SSADM and are managed under PRINCE.

1.2 Who should read this volume

This volume assumes that its readers either

- work in an environment in which it has already been decided to improve internal quality and management by implementing a quality system which conforms to ISO 9001

or

- require that their organisation's IS providers adhere to the requirements of ISO 9001.

Four classes of reader are addressed:

- providers of IS who manage their activities on development projects using PRINCE and use SSADM for the relevant analysis and design stages

- providers of IS who are planning to introduce PRINCE or SSADM for controlling their activities on IS development projects

- customers for IS or their representatives who wish to be sure that their suppliers have quality built into their production

- quality managers who wish to install a quality system at sites which are using SSADM with PRINCE for IS developments.

The volume is therefore likely to be of interest to:

- **managers responsible for IS development projects** who are required to advise or help quality managers in the setting up or maintaining a quality management system

- **managers and staff responsible for IS development projects that use PRINCE and SSADM** which are to satisfy the criteria of ISO 9001

- **project and stage managers** who are required to adhere to the criteria of ISO 9001

- **users of SSADM and PRINCE** who wish to understand the relevance of the method they work with to a quality management system

- **customers of IS organisations** who wish to check the extent to which their suppliers conform to ISO 9001

- **quality managers** who intend to install ISO 9001 conformant quality systems in sites that use SSADM with PRINCE for IS development projects.

1.3 Structure of this volume

Chapter 2 provides an overview of quality management for IS development projects and the background to the ISO 9001 family of quality standards.

Chapter 3 briefly describes PRINCE and SSADM together with their relationship to ISO 9001.

Chapter 4 examines the individual clauses of ISO 9001 and the extent to which they are satisfied by PRINCE and SSADM.

The check lists in the Annex are designed to help an auditor assess the conformance to ISO 9001 of a quality system which incorporates PRINCE and SSADM.

Chapter 1
Introduction

1.4 How to use this volume

This volume is written from the provider's perspective (as is ISO 9001) and is based on an organisational model in which the IS provider is an in-house IT directorate. Most of the guidance, however, applies irrespective of whether the provider is in-house or an external organisation. Readers who are customers for IS should substitute a "what should be done" view for the "what to do" perspective. Where IS providers and their customers are in different organisations it is anticipated that readers will encounter little difficulty in tailoring the guidance to suit their particular circumstances. The key considerations are the interfacing of the two organisations' quality systems and the extent to which the customer organisation requires that its policies should be adhered to by the provider.

This volume covers quality management for IS development projects only. Readers requiring information on quality generally or the setting up of a quality system should consult the Quality Management Library. Techniques which address various requirements of quality systems in relation to the provision of operational IT services may be found in the IT Infrastructure Library.

Readers who require an overview of the relationship of PRINCE and SSADM to quality standards should concentrate on Chapters 2 and 3. These readers are also likely to be interested in the check lists in the Annex.

Readers who are charged with implementing or maintaining a quality system, either as customers or suppliers, should concentrate on Chapter 4 and the Annex.

Readers who audit quality systems should refer to Chapter 4 and the Annex.

2 Quality Management for IS Development Projects

2.1 The importance of quality in IS development

In 1988 a study commissioned by the Department of Trade and Industry concluded that UK users and suppliers suffered software failure costs exceeding £500 million per year. The direct losses included costs for correcting software errors, overruns and unnecessarily high maintenance. The authors of the report were unable to quantify the "substantial" associated indirect costs.

Nowadays many IS providers have to compete for business. They must economically provide products and services of high quality to be competitive. The application of procedures within a quality system significantly reduces failure costs and contributes to effectiveness, efficiency and economy.

Equally, government departments as customers for IS need to be sure that they are obtaining value for money and limiting risk by choosing internal and external suppliers who are committed to providing quality products and services.

It is in the public interest that departments' internal and external suppliers are able to:

- provide low risk, high quality IS support for their customers' business operations
- provide value for money for their customers.

2.2 Quality system framework

A quality system comprises the organisational structure, responsibilities, procedures, processes and resources for implementing quality management. Within an IS provider's organisation, a quality system provides an enabling mechanism which coordinates and controls the functions needed to achieve the required quality of product or service in as effective, economic and efficient a way as possible.

Any quality system should:

- be flexible and adaptable
- prevent errors and waste
- be responsive to external and internal customer needs
- provide measures of process, product and service quality
- enable its users consistently to deliver products and services that meet the customers' needs
- be understood and effective.

CCTA recommends that providers of IS to government should have a quality system in place which ideally should conform to one of the international quality standards of the ISO 9000 series. In a market testing situation, however, customer organisations should at present guard against insisting on such conformance as it may unfairly restrict the number of potential providers.

Wherever possible, a quality system should be built on the framework of procedures and standards that already exists within the organisation. Where PRINCE is being used in conjunction with SSADM, much of the work needed to produce a documented quality system which conforms to ISO 9001 for IS development activities has already been done. However, a number of additional procedures such as those needed to ensure quality system effectiveness are required.

Figure 1 represents a quality system framework based on an organisation with an in-house IS provider. Where the customer and provider are in different organisations, frameworks similar to that shown in Figure 1 may apply to each. Agreement between the two parties must be reached on interfacing the frameworks and on customer policies that the provider will adhere to.

Chapter 2
Quality Management for IS Development Projects

The model on which the framework shown in Figure 1 is based is usually documented at three levels:

- organisation quality manual
- organisation-wide management manuals
- project, operational, administrative and technical manuals.

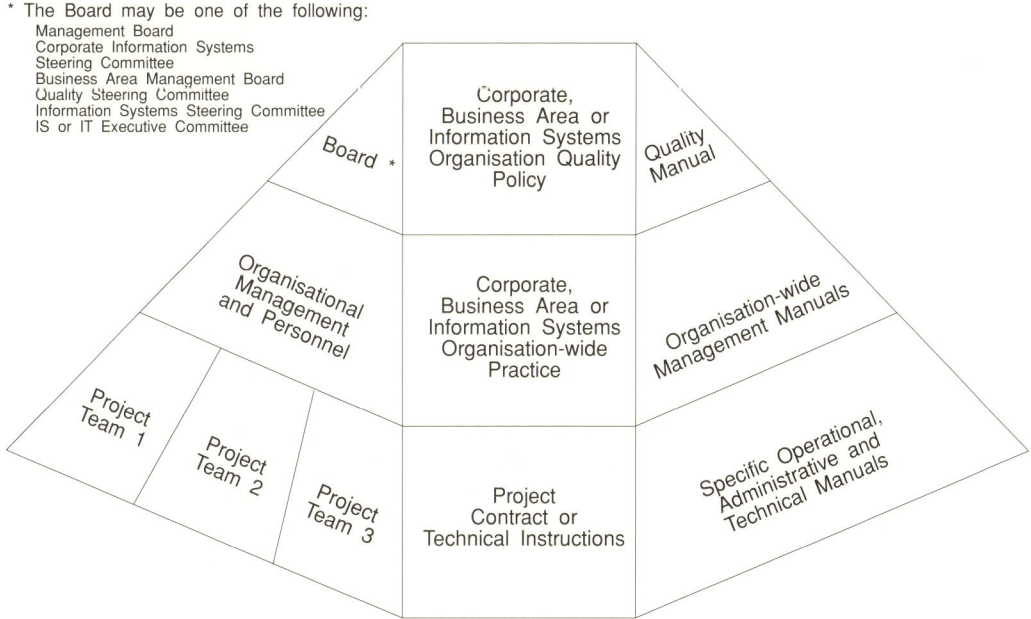

Figure 1: Quality system framework

The PRINCE and SSADM manuals sit at the middle level of this hierarchy. For IS development projects, the procedures associated with the use of PRINCE and SSADM address the middle level and the level below it.

The quality system is documented in an organisation's quality manual. This manual is the responsibility of the quality manager and typically includes:

- a statement of the quality policy
- the structure of the organisation together with individual responsibilities
- a definition of the various responsibilities for activities affecting quality
- policies, responsibilities and standards regarding individual activities laid down in ISO 9001
- an overview of the organisation's products and services
- specimen authorised signatures for final acceptance of products and services within the organisation
- document control for the quality manual
- glossary of terms.

Readers should consult the Quality Management Library for fuller details of the nature and implementation of a quality framework.

2.3 Quality standards

Customers need to be confident that their suppliers have quality built into their organisations. The way for a supplier to demonstrate this is to be able to prove that his organisation conforms to a recognised standard. It is for this reason that there has recently been an upsurge of interest in quality standards, particularly the international quality standard ISO 9001.

ISO 9001 is the international standard for quality systems, issued under the authority of the International Organisation for Standardization (ISO). It applies to quality assurance in design/development, production, installation and servicing.

There are two standards closely related to ISO 9001:

> ISO 9002, *covering production and installation but excluding design and development*

> ISO 9003, *covering only final inspection and test.*

In an IS environment these two standards may be relevant to such activities as outsourcing and facilities management. However, as they are both subsets of the main standard ISO 9001 they are not referred to specifically in the remainder of this volume.

There are two standards relating to the interpretation and application of ISO 9001:

> ISO 9000: *Quality systems - guide to selection and use.*

> ISO 9004: *Guide to quality management and quality system elements.*

Further such standards are in preparation.

There are equivalent British and European quality standards which are currently identical in wording to the international standard, although this may change in the future. The equivalence is:

International	British	European
ISO 9001	BS 5750 Part 1	EN29001
ISO 9002	BS 5750 Part 2	EN29002
ISO 9003	BS 5750 Part 3	EN29003

2.4 Certification

A quality certificate is a formal confirmation that an organisation's activities conform to ISO 9001, thereby giving a customer confidence in the effectiveness of his suppliers' quality systems. The certificate is awarded following a satisfactory quality audit by an independent external body.

Subsequently the certificate is subject to annual or biannual review audit; it must be renewed periodically by means of a full audit. For further details of certification, reference should be made to the Quality Management Library:

Quality Management System Audit

Quality Management Systems Implementation, Chapter 14.

Although anybody may carry out a quality audit, a certificate awarded by a body that has not been recognised as competent is of little or no value. Accreditation is the process whereby formal recognition of competence to carry out quality audits is given to a certification body. In the UK accreditation is vested with the President of the Board of Trade.

2.5 TickIT accreditation

ISO 9001 is a generic standard and until recently there were no generally accepted criteria for its interpretation for IS. The Department of Trade and Industry introduced the TickIT scheme in 1990 to:

- explain, for IS purchasers' benefit, the application of ISO 9001 to the production of software
- assist software providers by giving guidance in the use of ISO 9001
- clarify, for certification bodies, the interpretation of ISO 9001 with respect to software production
- set standards for the training of quality auditors.

TickIT addresses the ISO 9001 certification of quality systems used by organisations which develop software based IS. A set of guidelines (see bibliography) has been published which addresses those aspects of the quality system concerned with the specification, design, development, installation and support of computer software.

CCTA supports TickIT and recommends that any user or supplier of IS intending to obtain ISO 9001 certification stipulates that TickIT is included in the scope of certification and that the certification body is TickIT accredited. By so doing, they can be sure that their assessor is trained to audit software suppliers and their activities and systems. Details of certification bodies are available from the Institute of Quality Assurance, telephone 071 - 401 - 7227.

2.6 Definitions and terminology

Quality applies to two areas of production, the product itself and the processes which give rise to the product. The international standards vocabulary (ISO 8402) defines **quality** as:

The totality of features and characteristics of a product or service that bear on its ability to satisfy stated or implied needs.

Widely used informal interpretations of this definition are:

- **quality of a product** is its suitability for the purpose for which it is intended. Products include both services and tangible items

- **quality of a process** is its ability to deliver its products in a trouble free way.

A **procedure** is a formal definition of a process. This volume is concerned with how the component procedures of PRINCE and SSADM contribute to the achievement of both product and process quality.

The terms **validation** and **verification** have precise meanings within the context of ISO 9001. Their definitions are included in the glossary to this volume.

The terms **quality management system** and **quality system** are often used interchangeably. ISO 9001 uses the latter term as does this volume.

In this volume the SSADM conventions for the use of upper case letters have been adopted. Key planning and control documents such as *Product Description* have initial capitals, techniques such as *quality review* do not.

3 PRINCE and SSADM within a Quality System

3.1 Introduction

Quality management is concerned with the whole life of a product which typically may start with market research and end with disposal after use. A generic life cycle which may be applied to an information system is shown in Figure 2.

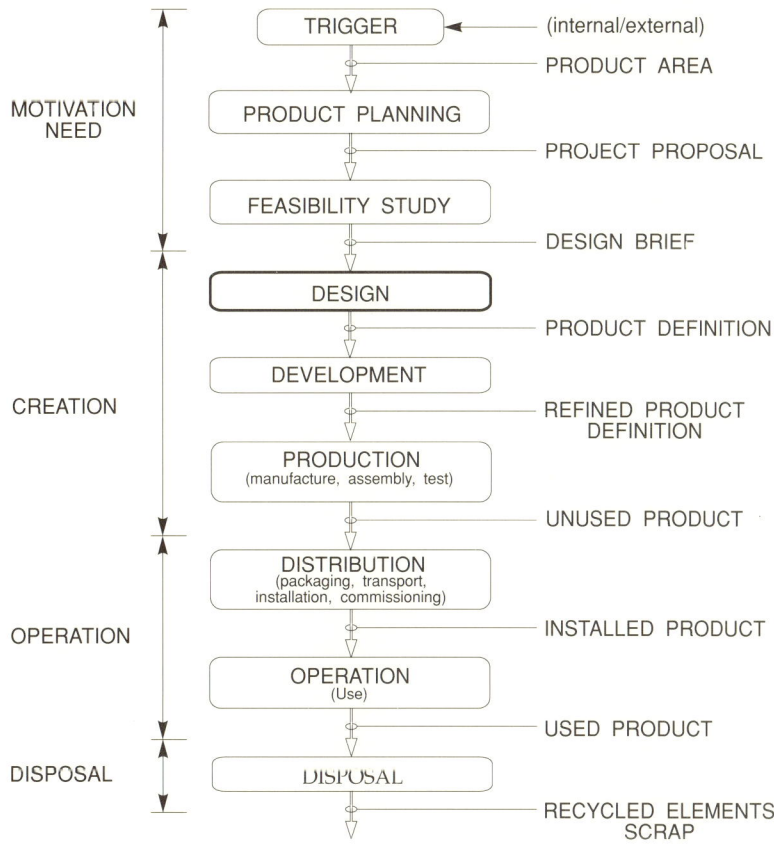

Source - BS7000: Guide to managing product design

Figure 2: A generic life cycle

CCTA recommends for IS projects that:

- activities which fall within the definition of a PRINCE project (see para 3.2) are managed using PRINCE

- SSADM is used under the control of PRINCE for analysis and design.

The adoption of this approach does not in itself produce conformance to the requirements of ISO 9001. For this to be achieved, further actions identified in Chapter 4 are required.

3.2   PRINCE   Projects in Controlled Environments (PRINCE) is a structured method for project management consisting of a set of procedures designed specifically for managing and controlling the planning, progress and quality of IS projects. Although PRINCE was developed for managing IS projects, it is based on general management principles and with informed tailoring can easily be adapted for the management of other types of project.

In PRINCE a project is regarded as having a defined and unique set of products, a set of activities to construct the products, appropriate resources to undertake the activities and a finite lifespan. PRINCE also requires an organisational structure with defined responsibilities. Within the context of the IS life cycle (Figure 2), PRINCE typically is used to control activities or the sub-activities which make them up, from feasibility study through production and installation. PRINCE does not specify the activities that a project should embrace. Thus more than one activity, e.g. design through production, may be controlled as one PRINCE project.

Other activities within the life cycle such as operation do not fall within the PRINCE definition of a project and are not controlled using PRINCE. However, many of the PRINCE procedures are relevant to the control of such activities but those procedures must be supplemented by further documented procedures and standards.

These further procedures and standards often already exist within an organisation and their introduction merely involves formally specifying and documenting them.

PRINCE is not and was not designed to be a comprehensive quality system. However three of its constituents contribute to a significant part of such a system. These are:

- quality controls which are clearly defined technical and management procedures

- product-based planning and the product descriptions which define the product quality criteria

- the PRINCE organisation (see Figure 3).

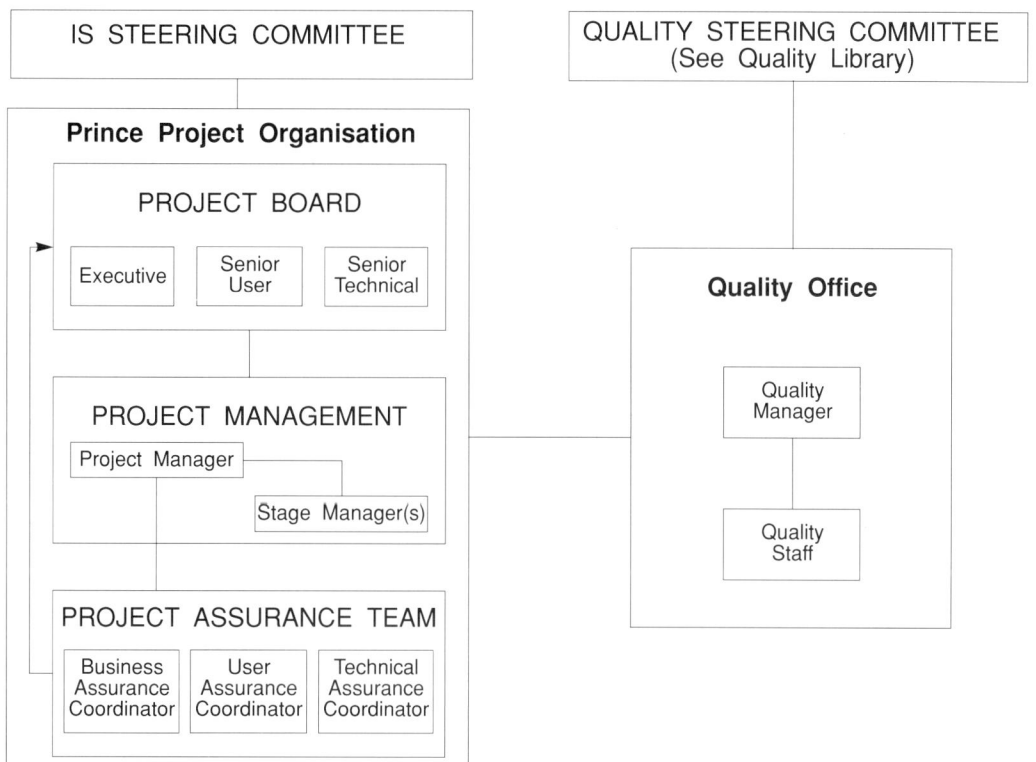

Figure 3: PRINCE organisation with its relationship to quality management

Because PRINCE is not in itself a quality system, its use does not automatically produce conformance to ISO 9001. To obtain conformance, further procedures need to be implemented and these are considered in Chapter 4.

3.3 SSADM

Structured Systems Analysis and Design Method (SSADM) is the UK Government's preferred method for use in the analysis and design of IS. It covers the activities from feasibility study through design. Version 4 of SSADM comprises five modules, each of which is made up of managed units of activity, stages and steps within stages.

Figure 4 illustrates how the various activities within SSADM Version 4 interface with PRINCE.

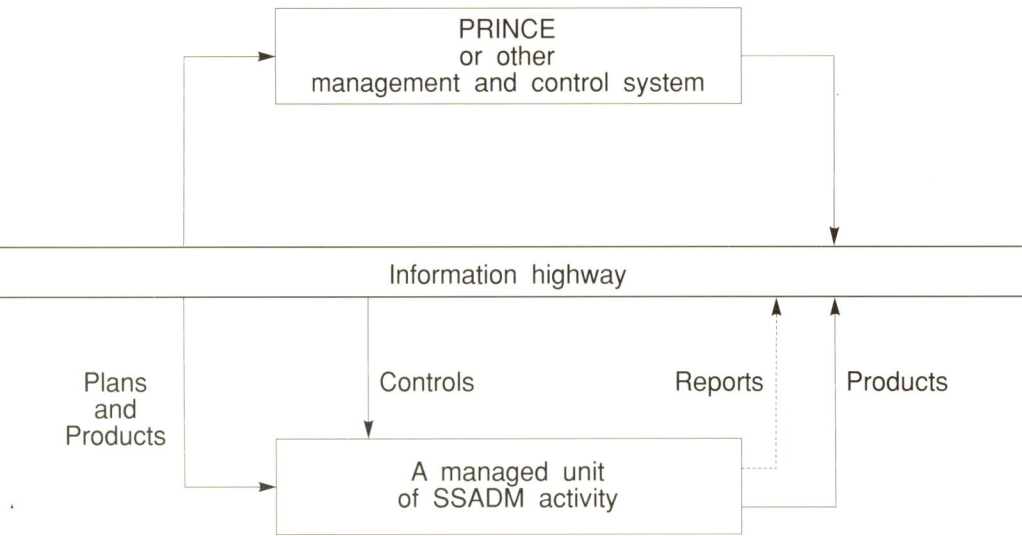

Figure 4: Interface between SSADM and PRINCE

CCTA recommends that the management and control mechanism is implemented by using PRINCE. A number of management procedures, such as quality reviews, are specified within the SSADM modules but controlled by the overall management mechanism.

All communication between SSADM and the project management, in the form of control mechanism, controls and products, must be via the information highway. Nothing may appear upon the information highway which does not satisfy the quality requirements both of the project management system and the relevant SSADM activity.

As with PRINCE, SSADM was not designed specifically to meet the requirements of ISO 9001. SSADM does, however, satisfy many of its requirements, for example:

- every product must be built to stated quality criteria (ISO 9001 requirement 4.4)
- all product versions are traceable back to the original requirement (ISO 9001 requirement 4.8).

4 The Requirements of ISO 9001

ISO 9001 prescribes what should be done within a quality system but it does not say how it should be done. For a quality system to conform to ISO 9001, it must satisfy each of the twenty clauses and associated sub-clauses of the standard relevant to the environment in which the quality system operates. In this chapter, the requirements are presented in the order in which they appear in ISO 9001 and in the following format:

1. The clause or sub-clause number and the requirement heading as it appears in the standard. The paragraph and sub-paragraph numbers of this chapter coincide with the clause numbers of ISO 9001.

2. A summary of the requirement.

3. In some cases, comments amplifying the requirement.

4. An account of the extent to which a project using SSADM and managed under PRINCE satisfies the requirement.

5. Pointers to further actions necessary to produce conformance with the requirement.

In addition to publications which are mentioned in connection with specific requirements of the standard, readers may find it useful to consult the following which are relevant to the whole of the standard:

- ISO 9004: *Quality Systems - Guide to quality management and quality system elements*
- Quality Management Library
- IT Infrastructure Library: *Quality Management for IT Services.* This volume is due for publication in September 1993.

4.1 Management Responsibility

4.1.1 Quality Policy

Requirement: The supplier's management shall define and document its policy with respect to quality.

Extent of conformance: This requirement is not addressed.

Further action: The quality policy must be set out in the quality manual in conformance with the requirements of ISO 9001. CCTA recommends that the quality policy include the use of PRINCE as the standard project management method with SSADM as the standard analysis and design method.

Chapter 4
The Requirements of ISO 9001

4.1.2 Organisation

4.1.2.1 Responsibility and authority

Requirement: The responsibility, authority and interrelation of all personnel who manage, perform and verify work affecting quality shall be defined. Particularly, personnel who need the organisational freedom and authority to:

- initiate action to prevent product nonconformity
- identify and record product problems
- initiate, recommend or provide solutions
- verify the implementation of solutions
- control further processing of a nonconforming product until the unsatisfactory condition has been corrected.

Extent of conformance: Within a project this requirement is fully satisfied. The PRINCE management guide contains detailed job descriptions for the various roles. A Project Initiation Document (PID) defines:

- specific responsibilities
- authorities
- interrelation of personnel.

SSADM defines in detail three roles to be filled for quality review, namely chairman, presenter and reviewer.

Further action: Responsibilities, authorities and interrelations of staff performing tasks affecting quality outside of projects must be defined and documented.

4.1.2.2 Verification resources and personnel

Requirement: The supplier shall identify in-house verification requirements and assign trained personnel for verification activities. Verification shall be carried out by personnel independent of those having direct responsibility for the work being performed.

Comment: The standard specifies that in this clause the term "verification" includes audits of the quality system as well as the definition given in the glossary to this volume. The requirement therefore also relates to objective evaluation of quality system elements. Areas of concern may include:

- organisational structures
- administrative and operational procedures
- personnel, equipment and procedures
- work areas, operations and processes
- items being produced
- documentation, reports and record keeping.

Extent of conformance: Within the context of projects, this requirement is addressed. Product Descriptions within both PRINCE and SSADM contain quality requirements, i.e. verification criteria for all products.

The most common form of verification mechanism is the quality review and the PRINCE Quality Plan contains details of the level of review and how the quality reviewers should be selected.

The project evaluation review and configuration audits provide input to audits of the quality system itself.

Chapter 4
The Requirements of ISO 9001

4.1.2 Organisation (continued)

Further action: Quality audit requirements for projects must be identified and suitably independent personnel appointed to carry them out.

Procedures relating quality system auditing beyond the confines of projects must be similarly defined.

ISO 10011 defines guidelines for auditing quality systems.

4.1.2.3 Management representative

Requirement: The supplier shall appoint a management representative who shall ensure that the requirements of the standard are implemented and maintained.

Extent of conformance: This requirement is not addressed.

Further action: A quality manager must be appointed and given the requisite authority. Depending on the size of the organisation, the quality manager may be full time and supported by a quality office.

4.1.3 Management review

Requirement: The quality system shall be reviewed at appropriate intervals to ensure its continuing suitability and effectiveness.

Extent of conformance: This requirement is not directly addressed. However, PRINCE project evaluation review reports and project files provide valuable and accessible sources of information to the staff reviewing the quality system. SSADM Stage files provide similar sources of information.

Further action: Formal procedures must be set up to review the effectiveness of the quality system.

4.2 Quality system

Requirement: The supplier shall establish and maintain a documented quality system as a means of ensuring that products conform to specified requirements. This shall include:

- the preparation of documented quality system procedures and instructions
- the effective implementation of the documented procedures and instructions.

Comment: Products must be produced in accordance with codes of practice declared by the supplier or in accordance with other specifications agreed between the supplier and customer.

Extent of conformance: This requirement is not addressed in full. PRINCE presents a framework of procedures and a model organisation structure that enforces adherence to procedures. SSADM is a code of practice for analysis and design. The adoption therefore of PRINCE in conjunction with SSADM contributes the major part of a quality system.

Further action: PRINCE may need tailoring to meet the specific needs of the organisation. Formal quality controls and standards need to be planned and documented.

Further procedures and standards which are required to satisfy ISO 9001 and which PRINCE and SSADM do not cover must be defined and documented as indicated in the remainder of this chapter.

4.3 Contract Review

Requirement: The supplier shall establish and maintain procedures for contract review. Each contract shall be reviewed by the supplier to ensure that:

- the requirements are adequately defined and documented
- any requirements differing from those in the tender are resolved
- the supplier is capable of meeting the contractual requirements.

Records of such contract reviews shall be maintained and review activities coordinated with the purchaser's organisation.

Comment: The purpose of this requirement is to ensure that the supplier and his sub-contractors are capable of doing the job before it is embarked upon. It applies to all types of contract, whether enforceable or not. Thus as well as applying to formal contracts it covers, for example, commitments made in respect of internal delivery of systems or services within an IT department.

Extent of conformance: This requirement is partially satisfied.

Where there is no formal contract, the acceptance of the PID by the project board is a confirmation of the supplier's ability to carry out the customers' requirements. If the project starts as a feasibility study, step 020 of SSADM ensures that the supplier's understanding of the requirements is synonymous with the requirements defined and documented in the contract. This is achieved by the supplier preparing a Problem Definition Statement in plain English and presenting it to the project board for approval. Any discrepancies arising during the review are resolved and signed off.

Chapter 4
The Requirements of ISO 9001

If the project does not start with a feasibility study, the PID is reviewed during SSADM step 110 of Stage 1 to ensure that the requirements are understood, clearly defined and capable of being achieved. Any significant problems are resolved with the project board before proceeding.

The monitoring and review of changing requirements is controlled in PRINCE by technical exception procedures.

PRINCE requires that the capability to deliver is established when the PID is accepted by the project board and thereafter kept under review. In the case of exceptions or deviations, the project board has authority to commit further resources to maintain the supplier's ability to deliver. The involvement of the senior user and the user assurance coordinator ensures liaison with the purchaser's organisation.

Further action: Where there is a formal contract, as between a software house and a customer or a supplier and sub-contractor, the supplier must carry out a documented contract review before any commitment is made.

4.4 Design Control

4.4.1 General

Requirement: The supplier shall establish and maintain procedures to control and verify the design of the product in order to ensure that the specified requirements are met.

Comment: This requirement relates to the translation of customer needs from the product brief into technical specifications for materials, products and processes. The specification and design should be such that the product or service is reproducible, verifiable and controllable. Quality plans form an important component of design control. Their requirements are amplified in paragraph 5 of ISO 9004: *Guide to quality management and quality system elements*.

Individual design control requirements are set down in the subsequent sub-paragraphs of paragraph 4.4.

Extent of conformance: All the requirements of this clause are satisfied or addressed as described in the following sub-paragraphs.

4.4.2 Design and development planning

Requirement: The supplier shall draw up plans to identify the responsibility for each design and development activity. Plans shall be updated as the design evolves.

Comment: Codes of practice or standards to be used must be defined.

Extent of conformance: This requirement is fully satisfied. Both PRINCE and SSADM define the management organisation and responsibilities and these are specified in the PID.

Updating of plans is under change control which is part of the configuration management system. Updating may occur as a result of:

- checkpointing
- stage planning prior to the start of a new Stage
- exception planning
- requests for change.

4.4.2.1 Activity assignment

Requirement: The design and verification activities shall be planned and assigned to qualified personnel equipped with adequate resources.

Extent of conformance: This requirement is partially satisfied. A complete structure for plans ranging from the whole project down to its SSADM stages is provided. The resource components of these plans specify in plain language the assignment of personnel. They also specify the necessary equipment and facilities.

Further action: Procedures must be enhanced to embrace relevant staff qualifications.

4.4.2 Design and development planning (continued)

4.4.2.2   Organisational and technical interfaces

Requirement: Organisational and technical interfaces between different groups shall be identified and the necessary information documented, transmitted and regularly reviewed.

Extent of conformance: This requirement is fully satisfied. The interfaces between groups and the job descriptions for the various PRINCE and SSADM roles are defined and documented in the PID.

The interfaces are reviewed at the following meetings:

- project initiation
- end stage assessments
- mid stage assessments
- project closure.

Chapter 4
The Requirements of ISO 9001

4.4.3 Design input

Requirement: Design input requirements relating to the product shall be identified and reviewed by the supplier. Incomplete, ambiguous or conflicting requirements shall be resolved with those responsible for drawing up the requirements.

Comment: Requirements for every design activity must be produced, reviewed and placed under configuration management. Each requirement must be so defined that its achievement is capable of verification. Design input requirements include:

- standards and methods to be used
- functional requirements
- design constraints, e.g. environmental and financial.

A design input is often a design output from a previous phase. Requirements for design outputs are stated in section 4.4.4.

Extent of conformance: This requirement is fully satisfied.

SSADM specifies the inputs to all its constituent steps. The SSADM Product Description for the Requirements Specification defines its content, form and quality criteria. All functional and non-functional requirements, including design constraints, are documented in the SSADM requirements catalogue. Resolution of incomplete, ambiguous or conflicting requirements is addressed during the requirement definition process and confirmed at quality review which is attended by the supplier and a representative of the user. Design requirements are under configuration management.

31

4.4.4 Design output

Requirement: Design output shall be documented and expressed in terms of requirements, calculations and analyses. Design output shall:

- meet the design input requirements
- contain or reference acceptance criteria
- conform to appropriate regulatory requirements
- identify those characteristics of the design that are crucial to the safe and proper functioning of the product.

Comment: There may be several phases of design, e.g. logical, physical and detailed, each phase of which generates a specification which in turn becomes the input to the next phase. Examples of requirements which may be included in calculations are:

- capacity planning data
- response times
- availability.

Extent of conformance: This requirement is partially satisfied.

Quality criteria within Product Descriptions must:

- define the need for products to conform to legislative requirements and meet the input design requirements
- include acceptance criteria.

SSADM ensures that design input matches the output from the previous phase.

Further action: Product Descriptions must specify any legal requirements and the characteristics that are required to ensure safe and proper functioning of the products.

4.4.5 Design verification

Requirement: The supplier shall plan, establish, document and assign to competent personnel functions for verifying the design. Design verification shall establish that design output meets the design input by means of appropriate control measures.

Appropriate control measures include:

- testing of models or prototypes
- comparing the new design with a similar proven one
- design reviews.

Comment: This clause is concerned with design approval procedures. A design should not normally be released to the production process until it has been properly approved. Release before approval, however, is acceptable under agreed controlled and documented conditions.

This requirement applies not only to reviews carried out at the end of each phase of design development. Examples of other categories of design review, see ISO 9004, for which a quality system should provide are:

- market readiness, to determine whether production capability and field support are adequate for a new or redesigned product
- design requalification to ensure that the design is still valid with respect to customer requirements.

Extent of conformance: This requirement is fully satisfied.

The requirement for a review to take place before a design product is released is identified within the Product Description. Quality criteria for each design product, the review method and the personnel functions or roles to be involved are also documented. Unless the defined quality criteria are met, a design is not accepted under configuration control.

Market readiness and design requalification are normally treated as projects in their own right and are controlled using PRINCE.

Chapter 4
The Requirements of ISO 9001

4.4.6 Design changes

Requirement: The supplier shall establish and maintain procedures for the identification, documentation and appropriate review and approval of all changes and modifications.

Extent of conformance: This requirement is fully satisfied.

The project issue, change control and configuration management procedures ensure that:

- the design, its input requirements and output criteria are all subject to change control
- proposed changes and their effects are subject to review and approval
- all aspects of design change are documented and approved.

4.5 Document Control

Requirement: The supplier shall establish and maintain procedures to control all documents and data that relate to the requirements of ISO 9001. These documents shall be reviewed for adequacy by authorised personnel prior to issue. The pertinent issues of the documents are to be available at all locations where operations are performed. Changes to documents shall be reviewed by the same functions that performed the original review unless specifically designated otherwise. Versions of documents are to be available where needed and obsolete copies promptly withdrawn.

Comment: This requirement applies to the documentation for the quality system itself as well as for projects. In the standard this clause is divided into two sub-clauses covering issue and changes.

Extent of conformance: This requirement is fully satisfied in respect of document control within a project. It is catered for by:

- document issue and withdrawal procedures in the PRINCE configuration management manual
- use of a standard PRINCE document header
- PRINCE change control procedures
- quality reviews of documents
- SSADM configuration management procedures.

Further action: Similar procedures are required for documentation outside of projects. These must include control of the standards and procedures within the quality system itself, e.g. change control and issuing procedures in respect of the corporate quality manual.

4.6 Purchasing

Requirement: The supplier shall ensure that purchased products conform to specified requirements.

Comment: This clause covers:

- the assessment of subcontractors (sub-clause 4.6.2)
- the need for purchasing documents to describe clearly the product ordered (sub-clause 4.6.3)
- verifying that any purchased product meets its specification (sub-clause 4.6.4).

Extent of conformance: Product Descriptions may include the requirements for purchasing documents, otherwise this requirement is not addressed by PRINCE nor SSADM.

Further action: The supplier must specify requirements in respect of purchased products in a way that facilitates subsequent verification of those products.

Verification may include assessment of a supplier's quality system.

4.7 Purchaser Supplied Product

Requirement: The supplier shall establish and maintain procedures for verification, storage and maintenance of purchaser supplied products.

Comment: This could be hardware or software provided by the customer for inclusion in his delivered system.

Extent of conformance: This requirement is not addressed.

Further action: Design reviews and testing requirements for purchaser supplied products must be defined and documented where appropriate. All such products must be placed under configuration management and procedures for software media and, if appropriate, hardware storage must be defined and documented.

Chapter 4
The Requirements of ISO 9001

4.8 Product Identification and Traceability

Requirement: Where appropriate, the supplier shall establish and maintain procedures for identifying the product from drawings, specifications or other documents during all stages of production, delivery and installation. Where traceability is specified, products shall have a unique identity.

Comment: It must be possible to identify all the products during design and development, how they are derived from other products and the products which are derived from them. Ultimately all products must be traceable back to the original requirement, including identification of when authorised changes have been made to the original requirement.

Traceability is achieved when it is possible to show:

- how any part of the requirement can be traced through the various stages of design and development to that part of the delivered system where the requirement is implemented

- how any part of the delivered system can be traced back to an agreed requirement.

Extent of conformance: This requirement is fully satisfied through:

- Product Breakdown Structures, Product Flow Diagrams and Product Descriptions which state the types of product to be produced, how they are derived and how they may be identified

- configuration management procedures which identify individual items and their relationship with other items

- change control procedures which ensure that any changes to requirement are properly authorised and reflected throughout all the relevant products

- the documentation requirements of SSADM which ensure that a product is traceable as it moves from one module or stage to the next.

Quality Management for PRINCE and SSADM Projects

Further action: The use of automated tools for systems analysis and design, code generation and configuration management greatly assists the achievement of this requirement. Procedures for verification and use of such tools must be available.

Chapter 4
The Requirements of ISO 9001

4.9 Process Control

Requirement: The supplier shall identify and plan the production and installation processes which directly affect quality and shall ensure that these processes are carried out under controlled conditions. Controlled conditions shall include:

- documented work instructions
- monitoring and control of process and product characteristics
- the approval of processes and equipment
- stipulating the criteria for workmanship.

Comment: A process accepts inputs, adds value to them and produces outputs. This clause is concerned with process management, that is ensuring that correct processes are conceived, used, monitored and updated. It is recognised in the standard (sub-clause 4.9.2) that there are special processes which cannot fully be verified by testing the product as faults may come to light only after the product has been in use. In such cases, continuous monitoring of the documented quality system is required to ensure that specified requirements are met.

Processes may apply at all stages of a product's development. They are also relevant to its replication, installation and maintenance.

Extent of conformance: Within a project as defined in PRINCE, this requirement is partially satisfied. Product Descriptions must include:

- reference to procedures, standards or working practices, i.e. documented work instructions, and to special processes
- quality criteria, i.e. criteria for workmanship.

41

Further action: All processes relevant to this clause must have documented work instructions. Processes and equipment must be approved and continually monitored. Within an IS development environment such processes include:

- the use of software tools including compilers and integrated project support environments (IPSEs) which must be put under configuration management

- the provision of centralised support services such as training and word processing

- the installation of the IS product

- software replication.

4.10 Inspection and Testing

4.10.1 Receiving inspection and testing

Requirement: The supplier shall ensure that an incoming product is not used until it has been inspected or otherwise verified as conforming to specified requirements. In cases of urgency the product may be used without such inspection provided it has been positively identified in case it needs to be recalled.

Comment: This clause refers to fitness for purpose of brought in components. Within an IS environment it often applies to software package evaluation and hardware acceptance procedures.

Extent of conformance: Where a product is being received as part of a project as defined in PRINCE then this requirement is satisfied. When the need for the incoming product has been identified, a Product Description is written which must specify the verification and testing required.

Further action: Hardware and software which is received outside of a project, e.g. one-off purchases, must be made subject to design verification and test. Procedures for identifying untested items must be defined and documented.

The following IT Infrastructure Library modules deal with this topic:

Computer Installation and Acceptance

Management of Local Processors and Terminals
Testing Software for Operational Use.

4.10.2 In-process inspection and testing

Requirement: The supplier shall:

- inspect, test and identify products as required in the quality plan or documented procedures
- establish product conformance to specified requirements by process monitoring and control methods
- hold products until the required inspection and tests have been completed
- identify nonconforming products.

Comment: Any product should be reviewed to demonstrate conformance to requirements before it is used in subsequent development phases of a project. Thus in software development, physical design should not start until the logical design has been successfully reviewed. The standard does however allow for *positive recall* in cases of urgency, whereby an unreviewed product may be used provided that it is positively identified so that it can be recalled should inspection subsequently show that it does not conform to requirements. Clearly this incurs a risk because correction costs would include not only the cost of correcting the product but also of products deriving from it.

Extent of conformance: This requirement is fully satisfied. Required tests, inspections and associated procedures are specified with the Product Descriptions. The Quality Plan is incorporated in the Stage Level Plans.

Both PRINCE and SSADM recommend the quality review as a mechanism for checking test results and the procedures for review are documented within the PRINCE quality guide. The objective of a quality review is to establish conformance to requirements, the results being recorded in the quality review result notification and follow-up action list.

Nonconforming products are positively and uniquely identified in the technical exceptions log. They may be identified in two ways:

- through outstanding errors following a quality review
- via the off-specification procedures.

4.10.3 Final inspection and testing

Requirement: The quality plan or documented procedure shall require that all specified reviews and tests are carried out before the product is released to a customer and that the associated data and documentation is available and authorised.

The supplier shall carry out final inspection and testing in accordance with the quality plan or documented procedures. No product shall be despatched until all the activities specified in the quality plan or documented procedures have been satisfactorily completed and associated data and documentation is available and authorised.

Comment: Within an IS environment this relates to:

- software replication
- system testing and demonstration
- customer acceptance testing.

Extent of conformance: This requirement is partially satisfied.

PRINCE (the documented procedures) and the project Quality Plan fully meet the requirement for system testing and customer acceptance testing. The quality review records provide evidence that all reviews have been carried out as specified in the quality plan.

The system acceptance letter is signed by the senior technical member of the project board before the system is released for customer acceptance testing. PRINCE ensures that acceptance letters are received by the supplier as evidence of a satisfied customer.

The method of acceptance testing, its specification, data and results are documented as Technical Products.

Further action: Procedures must be defined and documented for the distribution of replicated systems.

4.10.4 Inspection and test records

Requirement: The supplier shall establish and maintain records which give evidence that the product has passed inspection and test with defined acceptance criteria.

Extent of conformance: This requirement is partially satisfied.

The required records are held in the PRINCE quality file.

Further action: Retention periods for the various records must be defined.

4.11 Inspection, Measuring and Test Equipment

Requirement: The supplier shall control, calibrate and maintain inspection, measuring and test equipment.

Comment: This requirement does not apply to IS development processes *per se* although it does cover the calibration, checking and maintenance of test software.

Extent of conformance: This requirement is not addressed.

Further action: Readers are advised to consult ISO 9001 and BS 5781: *Measurement and Calibration Systems*.

Chapter 4
The Requirements of ISO 9001

4.12 Inspection and Test Status

Requirement: The inspection and test status of a product shall be identified in such a way as to indicate its conformance or nonconformance to inspections and tests. The identification of inspection and test status shall be maintained throughout production and installation.

Comment: The standard gives examples of identification methods including labels, inspection records and location.

Records should identify the inspection authority responsible for the release of conforming product.

Extent of conformance: This requirement is fully satisfied.

The following documents show the inspection status of documents and other products including software:

- quality review records
- Product Checklist
- graphical plan summary.

The authority for releasing a conforming product is the business assurance coordinator (BAC) or configuration librarian acting on the authority of the project manager or project board. He signs the quality review result notification and signs off any corrective follow-up action. All these documents are maintained in the PRINCE quality file.

Location of a product is under the control of the configuration management system.

4.13 Control of Nonconforming Product

Requirement: The supplier shall establish and maintain procedures to ensure that products not conforming to specified requirements are prevented from inadvertent use or installation. Controls shall provide for the identification and disposition of nonconforming products and for those concerned to be notified.

Comment: Nonconformance comprises products that have not been produced in conformance with requirements or procedures. Options (sub-clause 4.13.1) for dealing with nonconforming product include:

- reworking to meet the specified requirements
- accepting without repair (concession)
- use in alternative applications
- rejecting or scrapping.

Extent of conformance: This requirement is fully satisfied.

Nonconforming products are managed via the off-specification procedures, off-specification reports being raised as part of project issue reporting. The decision on disposition is documented and must be included in the user acceptance letter. This ensures that:

- the product is identified
- the problem is evaluated
- a properly authorised decision on disposition is made
- all relevant parties are notified.

The configuration status account allows the tracing of products that are affected by nonconformance.

Chapter 4
The Requirements of ISO 9001

4.14 Corrective Action

Requirement: The supplier shall establish, document and maintain procedures for:

- investigating the cause of nonconforming products

- analysing processes, work operations, concessions, quality records, service reports and customer complaints

- initiating and applying preventative actions to deal with problems

- implementing and recording changes to procedures.

Comment: This clause is concerned with the overall effectiveness of the quality system and is the concern of the quality office as much as project staff. In an IS development environment corrective action covers a system for reporting, recording and dealing with problems in the development and installation activities as revealed, for example, by failures in intermediate products. Examples are hardware and software errors arising during development and installation.

Extent of conformance: This requirement is not addressed.

PRINCE and SSADM do however provide valuable input to additional procedures through project records which include:

- quality review records

- Project Issue Reports

- change records

- Exception Plans

- reports and minutes of meetings

- project evaluation report

- corrective actions identified at quality reviews.

51

Further action: Procedures for reviewing and updating the quality system should be defined and documented.

4.15 Handling, Storage, Packaging and Delivery

Requirement: The supplier shall establish, document and maintain procedures for the handling, storage, packaging and delivery of products.

Extent of conformance: This requirement is not addressed.

Further action: Procedures must be defined and documented to cover the storage, handling and installation of products by the supplier or customer. This includes the storage by the supplier of master copies of software which has been replicated. For further details, see IT Infrastructure Library module: *Software Control and Distribution*.

Where a warranty applies, it must be clearly defined and communicated to the customer.

4.16 Quality Records

Requirement: The supplier shall establish and maintain procedures for the identification, collection, indexing, filing, storage, maintenance and disposition of quality records.

Quality records shall be maintained to demonstrate achievement of quality and the effective operation of the quality system.

All quality records must be legible and identifiable to the product concerned. They must be easily retrieved and stored in such a way as to prevent deterioration or loss. Retention times should be stated and, where required, the records should be made available to the customer.

Extent of conformance: This requirement is partially satisfied.

The project evaluation report gives some feedback on the effectiveness of technical and management procedures and standards.

Product quality records are available, principally within the project quality file, in the form of records of:

- what was planned, including quality requirements as specified in the product descriptions
- what was achieved, including the meeting of quality requirements and performance against planned schedules and budget
- product quality in terms of Quality Review documentation and Project Issues and their resolution
- overall product quality in terms of Acceptance Letters.

Chapter 4
The Requirements of ISO 9001

Further action: Procedures must be defined and documented which provide records demonstrating the effectiveness of the quality system. These records should include:

- internal and external quality audit documentation
- results of customer satisfaction surveys
- quality system change control documentation.

Retention periods, normally greater than one year from project closure, must be specified for quality records.

4.17 Internal Quality Audits

Requirement: The supplier shall carry out a comprehensive system of planned and documented internal quality audits to verify whether quality activities comply with planned arrangements and to determine the effectiveness of the quality system.

Comment: An audit is by definition carried out independently, normally by the quality office.

Extent of conformance: This requirement is not directly addressed.

Neither PRINCE nor SSADM includes audit procedures. However, both provide evidence which helps an auditor, particularly from:

- the quality criteria and documentary evidence of completed reviews
- project evaluation review and configuration audits
- the project assurance team's responsibility for ensuring that project specified quality controls are carried out and that standards are adhered to.

Further action: Audit procedures and schedules must be defined and documented. This topic is covered in depth by the Quality Management Library: *Quality Management System Audit*.

4.18 Training

Requirement: The supplier shall establish and maintain procedures for the identification of training needs and provide for the training of all personnel performing activities affecting quality. Appropriate records shall be maintained.

Extent of conformance: This requirement is not addressed.

The PRINCE framework of role descriptions, its requirement for job descriptions and the detailed Product Descriptions do, however, assist the supplier in identifying training needs.

Because each SSADM technique is used at a specific point within the analysis and design phases, it is possible to draw up a skills profile for those parts of the project.

Further action: Procedures must be defined and documented which identify the need and provide for training.

It must be possible in all cases to demonstrate that a minimum skill level has been acquired and proper training records must be kept.

4.19 Servicing

Requirement: Where servicing is specified in the contract, the supplier shall establish and maintain procedures for performing and verifying that servicing meets the specified requirements.

Comment: Within an IS environment this requirement refers to maintenance, including error correction, changes or enhancements and problem resolution.

Extent of conformance: As this activity comes within service delivery, it is not directly addressed by PRINCE which assumes a finite project life. Similarly, SSADM does not concern itself with servicing. As was pointed out in Chapter 3, however, these types of activity, including maintenance projects, may be managed using procedures of PRINCE and techniques of SSADM supplemented by further procedures and standards.

Further action: The required supplementary procedures depend on the nature of the servicing being carried out. Typically they need to:

- provide the ability to control and measure response and service recovery times
- ensure the protection of customers' data
- define, in cases where there is a range of service options, what they are and where and in what circumstances they are provided
- define processes for installation of additional hardware or software
- define the period for which the service is available.

Chapter 4
The Requirements of ISO 9001

For fuller details, refer to *Guide to Software QMS Construction and Certification using ISO 9001* (TickIT manual) and IT Infrastructure Library modules:

Change Management

Help Desk

Problem Management
Service Level Management

4.20 Statistical Techniques

Requirement: Where appropriate, the supplier shall establish procedures for identifying adequate statistical techniques for verifying the acceptability of process capability and product characteristics.

Comment: This requirement applies in two areas:

- the statistical techniques themselves, e.g. quality metrics
- applying the techniques, e.g. with a view to improving quality.

Extent of conformance: This requirement is not directly addressed.

The following data suitable for statistical analysis is however available from the project evaluation review:

- types of technical exceptions arising and when they happened
- details of errors identified in quality reviews
- actual expenditure and resource usage together with comparisons against estimates.

Further action: Where relevant, appropriate statistical techniques must be identified and applied. This is a complex subject to which the International Organisation for Standardization has produced codes of practice including:

- ISO Standards Handbook 3: *Statistical Methods*
- ISO 3534: *Statistics - vocabulary and symbols*
- publications of ISO Technical Committee 56, the full list of titles may be obtained from BSI.

Annex: The Relationship of PRINCE and SSADM to ISO 9001

Chapter 4 is written from the viewpoint of how an IS project which is controlled by PRINCE and uses SSADM addresses the requirements of ISO 9001. For the convenience of readers, this annex lists the contributions of PRINCE and SSADM separately.

The annex contains three tables:

1. A summary of the extent to which PRINCE and SSADM each satisfies the requirements of ISO 9001.

2. The main elements of PRINCE which are relevant to the various requirements of ISO 9001.

3. The main elements of SSADM which are relevant to the various requirements of ISO 9001.

The following abbreviations are used in Table 1:

S - PRINCE or SSADM satisfies the requirement.

A - PRINCE or SSADM addresses the requirement but does not fully satisfy it.

N - PRINCE or SSADM does not address the requirement directly.

Clause	PRINCE	SSADM
4.1 Management Responsibility		
4.1.1 Quality policy	N	N
4.1.2 Organisation		
4.1.2.1 Responsibility & authority	A	A
4.1.2.2 Verification resources etc	A	A
4.1.2.3 Management representative	N	N
4.1.3 Management review	N	N
4.2 Quality System	A	A
4.3 Contract Review	A	A
4.4 Design Control		
4.4.1 General		
4.4.2 Design & development planning	S	S
4.4.2.1 Activity assignment	A	A
4.4.2.2 Organisational interface	S	S
4.4.3 Design input	S	S
4.4.4 Design output	A	A
4.4.5 Design verification	S	S
4.4.6 Design changes	S	S
4.5 Document Control	A	A
4.6 Purchasing	A	N
4.7 Purchaser Supplied Product	N	N
4.8 Product Identification & Traceability	S	S
4.9 Process Control	A	N
4.10 Inspection and Testing		
4.10.1 Receiving	A	N
4.10.2 In-process	S	A
4.10.3 Final	A	N
4.10.4 Records	A	N
4.11 Test Equipment	N	N
4.12 Inspection & Test Status	S	N
4.13 Control of Nonconforming Products	S	N
4.14 Corrective Action	N	N
4.15 Handling, Storage, Package, Delivery	N	N
4.16 Quality Records	A	A
4.17 Internal Quality Audits	N	N
4.18 Training	N	N
4.19 Servicing	N	N
4.20 Statistical Techniques	N	N

Table 1: The Extent to which PRINCE and SSADM Satisfy the Requirements of ISO 9001

Clause	Relevant PRINCE Element
4.1 Management Responsibility	
4.1.1 Quality policy	None
4.1.2 Organisation	
4.1.2.1 Responsibility & authority	PRINCE roles
4.1.2.2 Verification resources etc	Product Descriptions
	Stage Plans
	Quality Plan
4.1.2.3 Management representative	None
4.1.3 Management review	Project evaluation review
4.2 Quality System	The whole method
4.3 Contract Review	Project initiation meeting
	Checkpoints
	Stage Assessments
	Exception Plans
4.4 Design Control	
4.4.1 General	See below
4.4.2 Design & development planning	Project Initiation Document
	Product Descriptions
	Plans
	Change control
4.4.2.1 Activity assignment	Plans
4.4.2.2 Organisational interface	Project Initiation Document
	PRINCE roles
	Product Flow Diagram
	Reports
	Meetings
4.4.3 Design input	Product Descriptions
	Quality review
	Configuration management
4.4.4 Design output	Product Descriptions
4.4.5 Design verification	Product Descriptions
	Quality review
4.4.6 Design changes	Project issue reports
	Configuration management
	Change control
4.5 Document Control	Configuration management
	Change control
4.6 Purchasing	Product Descriptions

Table 2: The Main Elements of PRINCE which are Relevant to the Requirements of ISO 9001

Clause	Relevant PRINCE Element
4.7 Purchaser Supplied Product	None
4.8 Product Identification & Traceability	Product Breakdown Structures
	Product Flow Diagrams
	Product Descriptions
	Configuration management
	Change control
4.9 Process Control	Product Descriptions
4.10 Inspection and Testing	
4.10.1 Receiving	Product Descriptions
4.10.2 In-process	Product Descriptions
	Quality plan
	Quality reviews
4.10.3 Final	Quality reviews
	Acceptance letter
	Technical Product Descriptions
4.10.4 Records	Quality records
4.11 Test Equipment	None
4.12 Inspection & Test Status	Quality records
	Product check list
	Graphical plan summary
	Configuration management
4.13 Control of Nonconforming Products	Off-specification Reports
	Project Issue Reports
	Acceptance letter
4.14 Corrective Action	Project records
4.15 Handling, Storage, Package, Delivery	Technical Product Descriptions
4.16 Quality Records	Quality records
4.17 Internal Quality Audits	None
4.18 Training	PRINCE roles
4.19 Servicing	None
4.20 Statistical Techniques	Project evaluation review

Table 2: The Main Elements of PRINCE which are Relevant to the Requirements of ISO 9001 (continued)

Annex
The Relationship of PRINCE and SSADM to ISO 9001

Clause	Relevant SSADM Element
4.1 Management Responsibility	
4.1.1 Quality policy	None
4.1.2 Organisation	
4.1.2.1 Responsibility & authority	SSADM roles
4.1.2.2 Verification resources etc	Product Descriptions
	Quality reviews
4.1.2.3 Management representative	None
4.1.3 Management review	Stage files
4.2 Quality System	Quality control
	Configuration management
4.3 Contract Review	Problem Definition Statement
	Project Initiation Document
4.4 Design Control	
4.4.1 General	See below
4.4.2 Design & development planning	SSADM roles
	Product Descriptions
	Requests for change
	Exception plans
4.4.2.1 Activity assignment	Plans
4.4.2.2 Organisational interface	SSADM roles
	Reports
	Defined meetings
4.4.3 Design input	Requirements Catalogue
4.4.4 Design output	Quality reviews
4.4.5 Design verification	Requirements Catalogue
4.4.6 Design changes	Configuration management
4.5 Document Control	Configuration management
4.6 Purchasing	None
4.7 Purchaser Supplied Product	None
4.8 Product Identification & Traceability	Product Descriptions
	Product Breakdown Structures
	Configuration management
	Change control
4.9 Process Control	None

Table 3: The Main Elements of SSADM which are Relevant to the Requirements of ISO 9001

Clause	Relevant SSADM Element
4.10 Inspection and Testing	
4.10.1 Receiving	None
4.10.2 In-process	Quality reviews
4.10.3 Final	None
4.10.4 Records	None
4.11 Test Equipment	None
4.12 Inspection & Test Status	None
4.13 Control of Nonconforming Products	None
4.14 Corrective Action	Project records
4.15 Handling, Storage, Package, Delivery	None
4.16 Quality Records	Quality reviews
4.17 Internal Quality Audits	Quality reviews
4.18 Training	Product Descriptions
4.19 Servicing	None
4.20 Statistical Techniques	None

Table 3: The Main Elements of SSADM which are Relevant to the Requirements of ISO 9001 (continued)

Bibliography

Information Systems Guide	The Information Systems Guides, published by CCTA, are available from John Wiley & Sons Ltd, Baffins Lane, Chichester PO19 1UD.
IT Infrastructure Library	The IT Infrastructure Library volumes are available from HMSO Publications Centre, PO Box 276, London SW8 5DT.
Quality Management Library	The Quality Management Library volumes are available from HMSO Publications Centre, PO Box 276, London SW8 5DT.
TickIT documentation	TickIT documentation is available from DTI TickIT Project Office, 8 Newman Street, London W1A 4SE. Telephone (071) 3834501.
British Standard and ISO documentation	The British and International standards are available from the British Standards Institute, Linford Wood, Milton Keynes, MK14 6LE. Telephone (0908) 221166, telex (0908) 825777.
Other publication	Software Quality Standards: The Costs and Benefits. A review for the Department of Trade and Industry, Price Waterhouse, April 1988.

Glossary

audit	See *quality audit*
BS	British Standard
BSI	British Standards Institute
concession or waiver	Written authorization to use or release a quantity of material, components or stores already produced but which do not conform to the specified requirements. [ISO 8402]
ISO	International Organisation for Standardization.
ITIL	Information Technology Infrastructure Library. CCTA guidance on infrastructure management.
nonconformity	The non-fulfillment of specified requirements. [ISO 8402]
procedure	A formal definition of a process.
PID	Project Initiation Document.
process	Any activity that accepts inputs, adds value to these inputs for customers and produces outputs for those customers. The customers may be either internal or external to the organisation. [BS 4891]
quality	The totality of features and characteristics of a product or service that bear on its ability to satisfy stated or implied needs. [ISO 8402]

Informal interpretations of this definition are:

- Quality of a product is its suitability for the purpose for which it is intended. Products include both tangible items and services
- Quality of a process is its ability to deliver its products in a trouble free way.

quality audit	A systematic and independent examination to determine whether quality activities and related results comply with planned arrangements and whether these arrangements are implemented effectively and are suitable to achieve objectives. [ISO 8402]
Quality Management Library	CCTA advice on improving quality awareness, knowledge and practice within government IS departments and agencies.
quality system	The organizational structure, responsibilities, procedures, processes and resources for implementing quality management. [ISO 8402]
supplier	An organisation which designs, develops, installs and maintains products to meet requirements specified by the customer. The customer may be external or internal to the supplier's organisation.
TickIT	The UK Department of Trade and Industry initiative supporting the improvement and promotion of third party certification of software quality systems for conformance with BS 5750/ISO 9001.
validation	In the context of ISO 9001, the process of checking the finished product for conformance to specified requirements before it is released to the customer.
verification	In the context of ISO 9001, the process of checking, as design and development progresses, the quality of the results of one phase of work before moving onto the next.